AF584303

For my sweetheart and my cubs — J.P.

For Vinita and Digby — R.G.

Scholastic Press
An imprint of Scholastic Australia Pty Limited (ABN 11 000 614 577)
PO Box 579 Gosford NSW 2250
www.scholastic.com.au

Part of the Scholastic Group
Sydney • Auckland • New York • Toronto • London • Mexico City
New Delhi • Hong Kong • Buenos Aires • Puerto Rico

Published by Scholastic Australia in 2022.

A catalogue record for this book is available from the National Library of Australia

ISBN: 978-1-76112-630-7

Typeset in Old Claude LP.
Design by Sofya Karmazina.

Ronojoy Ghosh created these illustrations digitally.

Printed in China by RR Donnelley.
Scholastic Australia's policy, in association with RR Donnelley, is to use papers that are renewable and made efficiently from wood grown in responsibly managed forests, so as to minimise its environmental footprint.

10 9 8 7 6 5 22 23 24 25 26 / 2

FAMILY TREE
Josh Pyke
Ronojoy Ghosh
A Scholastic Press book from Scholastic Australia

It started with a seed,
and that seed was me.

I grew day by day

as red bricks were laid.

My roots dug deep
as the walls climbed
to meet a red roof
with a chimney on top.

And, over time,
laughter filled my garden.

Little hands reached higher and higher,
leaving little scars in my trunk.

A heart,
an arrow.

Seasons came and went . . .

feast and famine,

drought and storms.

Laughter,

tears,

silence,

song.

YES

Our roots dug deeper.
Our roots grew strong.

Until, one day,

those little hands grew
too big for my branches.

I was outgrown.

1885
889
LAUNDRY
LAUNDRY AND DRY CLEAN
PHO ★ VIET
VIET
BEST

So, for a time, they were gone,
to grow their own trees,
in their own gardens.

LEWISHAM
公共交通
票务票价
SERVIC
DOG

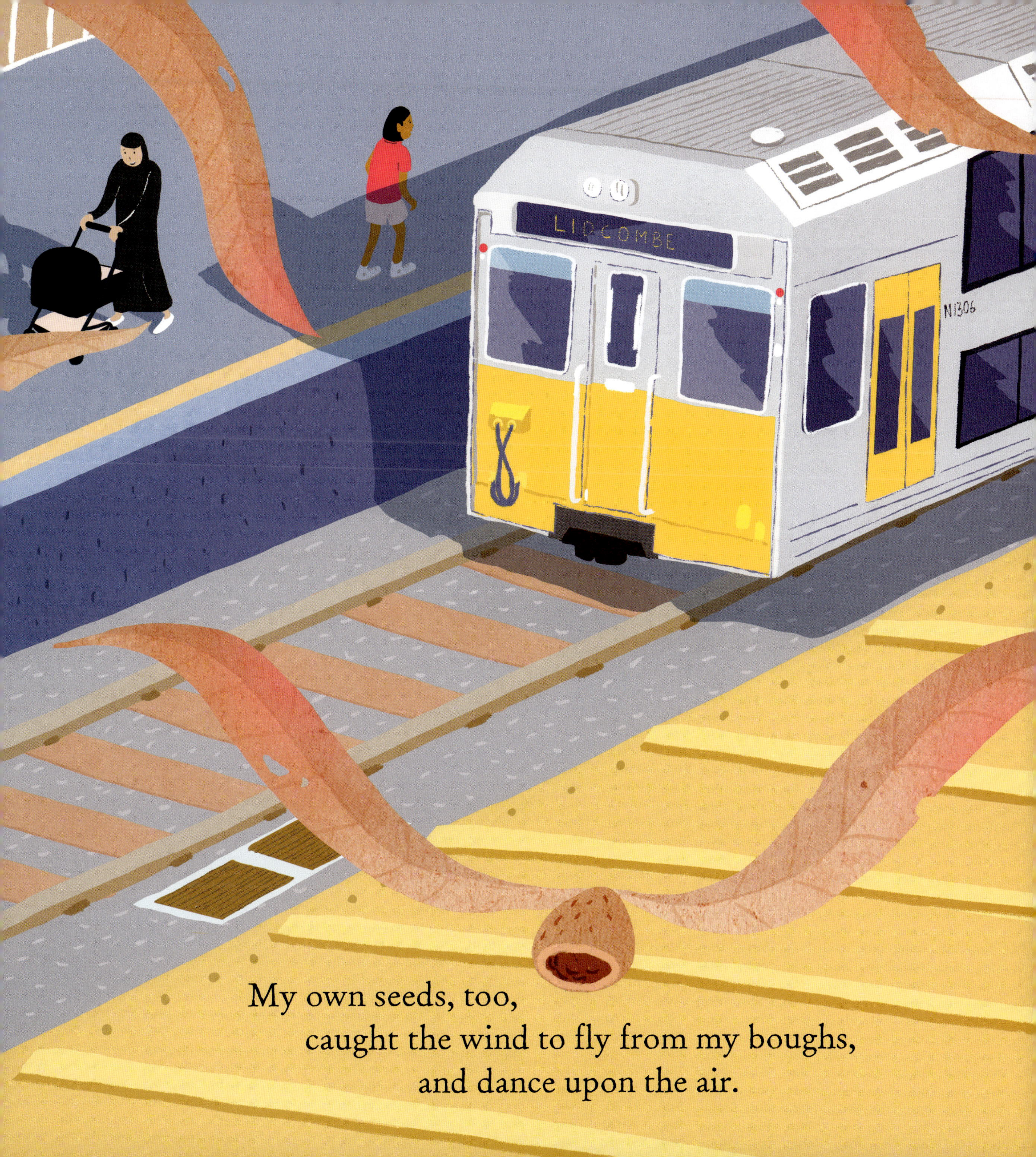

My own seeds, too,
caught the wind to fly from my boughs,
and dance upon the air.

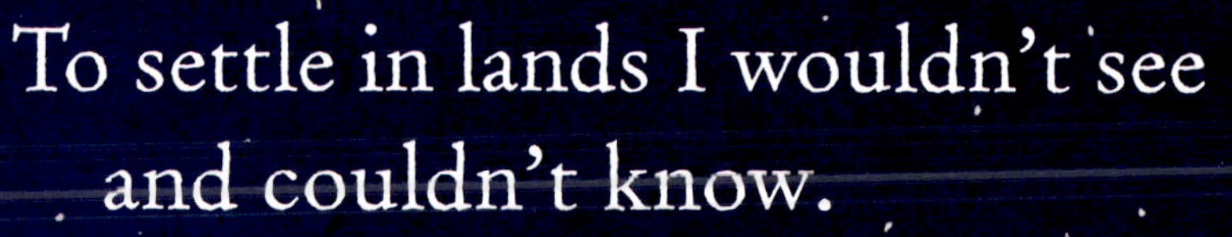

To settle in lands I wouldn't see
and couldn't know.

Forever away.
Forever my own.

But then, in bursts, like flashes
of brilliant golden light,

little laughter returned,
little voices.

‘A heart!’ they sang.
‘An arrow!’

Little hands, brand new,
but known.

New scars, too,
that hurt not one little bit.

And my branches were strong
under those little hands.

My boughs wide under those
little feet, those little lives.

I grew again.
I reached my branches toward the sun
so that they could climb higher.

Ever higher.

And they did.

They climbed all the way to the sky.

It started with a seed,

and that seed was *me*.